CW01020484

PRAYERFUL HOUR

A Scriptural Companion
to Eucharistic Adoration

Fr Florian Racine

*All booklets are published
thanks to the generosity of the supporters
of the Catholic Truth Society*

All rights reserved. First published 2018 by The Incorporated Catholic Truth Society 40-46 Harleyford Road London SE11 5AY Tel: 020 7640 0042 Fax: 020 7640 0040. © 2018 The Incorporated Catholic Truth Society.

Original edition Could You Not Watch with Me One Hour? *© 2014, Ignatius Press. Reprinted with permission. All rights reserved.*

ISBN 978 1 78469 203 2

Contents

STAGE 1

Introduction to the Itinerary

In his last encyclical, Pope John Paul II wrote:

> The mystery of the Eucharist – sacrifice, presence, banquet – *does not allow for reduction or exploitation*; it must be experienced and lived in its integrity, both in its celebration and in the intimate converse with Jesus which takes place after receiving communion or in a prayerful moment of Eucharistic adoration apart from Mass. These are times when the Church is firmly built up and it becomes clear what she truly is: one, holy, catholic and apostolic; the people, temple and family of God; the body and bride of Christ, enlivened by the Holy Spirit; the universal sacrament of salvation and a hierarchically structured communion ... The treasure of the Eucharist, which the Lord places before us, impels us towards the goal of full sharing with all our brothers and sisters to whom we are joined by our common baptism.[1]

| *Holy Sacrifice* | *Holy Communion* | *Adoration of the Blessed Sacrament* |

6

- What are the three dimensions of the Eucharistic mystery?

- What is the meaning of the two terms "mystery" and "treasure" that John Paul II uses for the Eucharist?

- "The Eucharist builds the Church and the Church makes the Eucharist." (*Ecclesia de Eucharistia*, no.26)

- What are the names given to the Church?

- "The treasure of the Eucharist…impels us towards [its] full sharing." Just what is this?

Here, the term "mystery" designates an effective action and presence of God in the Church, for the life of the world and the sanctification of souls. The "mystery" exceeds the intellect without, however, contradicting it. Jesus is really present in the Eucharist. All the sacraments are acts of Christ through which he gives us his grace. But, in the Eucharist, he is there himself, permanent, living, and acting, hidden under the appearances of the sacred Host. The itinerary will present the divine life of Jesus in the Blessed Sacrament, what he does there and what he expects of us. The word "treasure" reminds us that the Eucharist is our greatest treasure. St Augustine, in speaking of God, wrote about the Eucharist: "All-powerful that he is, he could make nothing greater; all-wise that he is, he could find nothing more admirable; all-wealthy that he is, he could not make a more precious present."

In other words, God cannot give us a greater gift than that of the Eucharist. In his omnipotence, he cannot bear greater witness to his love. He has nothing greater to offer. St Peter Julian Eymard said: "Happy the soul that knows how to find Jesus in the Eucharist and, in the Eucharist, all things."[2] Through the Eucharist, we enter into the great movement of love: "From the heights of the Trinity, the incarnate Word descends to man in the Eucharist in order that, through Communion, man may ascend to his final end, the most-lovable Trinity."[3]

Eucharistic grace "impels us towards…the full sharing…" of this treasure. In the context of the encyclical, the concern is the communal celebration of the Eucharist between all Christians who have received the same baptism. To arrive at this goal, we must work towards the re-establishment of full ecclesial communion. But we can understand it more broadly: we cannot keep this treasure for ourselves: on the one hand, it has to be announced to all, and, on the other, it has to drive us to give ourselves to others as Christ handed himself over for us. *Evangelisation* and *charity*, these are the two dimensions of the Church's mission.

Through different stages founded on biblical texts, the itinerary will present what the Eucharist is, what is fulfilled in the Holy Mass, what Communion and adoration are, and why and how to adore, for "true worshippers will worship the Father in spirit and truth, for such the Father seeks to worship him" (*Jn* 4:23). Through illustrations, Magisterial texts, and quotations from the saints, the adorer will discover how to enter into the following movement: in adoring the Son, to be driven towards the Father to receive the Holy Spirit and thus become a missionary, by announcing this treasure and by sharing the charity that flows from it. And all this in the Church, who gives us the Eucharist and who lives from the Eucharist. The itinerary will also stress the spiritual attitudes required for entering into adoration "in spirit and truth" as well as the practical means for remaining faithful to prayer, despite inevitable times of dryness and purification. The adorer will learn to draw from this "spring of water welling up to eternal life" (*Jn* 4:14), which comes from the Eucharistic Heart of Jesus.

Each stage can be made during or after the weekly hour of adoration, with the aid of the Bible. It is a self-taught course, a school of adoration offered to every believer. Those responsible for adoration in a parish will be able to have successive evaluations with the adorers of their staff in order to clarify certain points or respond to their potential questions. Here is the outline of the itinerary offered:

• *Introduction* (*one stage:* the three dimensions of the Eucharist).

The Father: Through the Son, Ascending to the Father and Letting Oneself Be Transformed by His Love (*ten stages*):

• *He Is the Good Shepherd Who Leads Me to the Father* (*allowing oneself to love*) (*five stages:* Cain's and Abel's offerings and the offering of oneself; "the Lord is my shepherd", the evangelisation of my being; "the clay in the potter's hands"; "Not what I will, but what you will"; "Abba, Father", adoration: remedy for pride and despair).

• *Spiritual Warfare* (*from sensible graces to the adoration of the Father "in spirit and truth"*) (*five stages:* "Be still, and know that I am God"; Jacob's struggle and spiritual advice; the trial of the wilderness [adoration in battle, recollection, contemplation]; Moses fights against the Amalekites, and the paralytic: the power of intercession; "a prophet is without honour in his own country").

HE IS THE GOOD SHEPHERD WHO LEADS ME TO THE FATHER

STAGE 2

Cain's and Abel's Offerings
The Offering of Oneself

Now Abel was a keeper of sheep, and Cain a tiller of the ground. In the course of time Cain brought to the Lord an offering of the fruit of the ground, and Abel brought some of the firstlings of his flock and of their fat portions. And the Lord had regard for Abel and his offering, but for Cain and his offering he had no regard. So Cain was very angry, and his countenance fell. The Lord said to Cain, "Why are you angry, and why has your countenance fallen? If you do well, will you not be accepted? And if you do not do well, sin is lurking at the door; its desire is for you, but you must master it." Cain said to Abel his brother, "Let us go out to the field." And when they were in the field, Cain rose up against his brother Abel, and killed him. (*Gn* 4:2-8)

No reason is indicated to justify the Lord's preference: it depends on his free will. Cain's subsequent attitude manifests the bad disposition of his heart. This mysterious passage can enlighten us about our adoration. The Lord did not have regard for Cain's offering. For Cain worships God, but he keeps one eye on his brother; his heart is not entirely God's. God sees first the person, the heart, and not the offering. Later, the Lord will say to Samuel:

Do not look on his appearance or on the height of his stature, because I have rejected him; for the Lord sees not as man sees; man looks on the outward appearance, but the Lord looks on the heart. (*1 S* 16:7)

Adoration brings us into the truth. It turns us entirely to our Father by decentring us from ourselves. It is about giving to God the worship that is his by right: "You shall worship the Lord your God and him only shall you serve" (*Mt* 4:10). This implies adoring God as the Lord of all that exists; giving him the worship due to him individually and communally; praying to him with praise, thanksgiving, and supplication; offering sacrifices to him – above all, the spiritual sacrifice of our life – united to the perfect sacrifice of Christ. In the parable of the Pharisee and the Publican, the Pharisee offers his good acts, while the tax collector humbly presents his own life to God, despite its flaws. Jesus declares: "This man went down to his house justified rather than the other" (*Lk* 18:9-14).

When we come to adore Jesus in the Blessed Sacrament, we present ourselves to him as we are truly! His presence frees us, heals us, and establishes us in the truth. We can then order our life in God's light and let ourselves be put at peace. This will be reflected in our behaviour towards our brothers. St Paul encourages us to offer our bodies to God. This is the true spiritual worship that leads to conversion of the heart. This "transformation" consists in renewing our judgement in order to discern the will of God in all things: "I appeal to you therefore, brethren, by the mercies of God, to present your bodies as a living sacrifice, holy and acceptable to God, which is your spiritual worship. Do not be conformed to this world but be transformed by the renewal of your mind, that you may prove what is the will of God, what is good and acceptable and perfect" (*Rm* 12:1-2). Adoration, when it becomes the offering of oneself renews one's way of thinking and judging. Changing one's way of looking at others, the world, and oneself makes us receptive to welcoming the divine will: this is true conversion. For it, one must abandon oneself entirely to the Lord and even die to oneself.

For St Thérèse of Lisieux, "the nature of love is to humble oneself… In order that Love be fully satisfied, it is necessary that It lower Itself… to nothingness and transform this nothingness into *fire*."[4] Sister Marie-Thérèse Dubouché said: "Eucharistic adoration is being there like a flower before its sun. If you knew who it is who watches you through these veils… Do nothing, no matter what! A virtue will come forth from him."[5]

Here is the testimony of an adorer who, through a very serious illness, carries the world by her heroic offering:

Is life worth living? This is what I was asking myself in 1998 when, at the age of thirty-three, I was informed that I would live all my life in palliative care, but with a normal life expectancy, with the sciatic nerve alive, in unceasing pain day and night that even continual infusions of morphine are insufficient to relieve. It was in adoration and offering of myself that I found the answer to this question. I discovered adoration during a retreat. From questioning I passed to marvelling: I had entered into adoration. That day in March 1998, I received the grace of a vital need to meet Jesus each day in the Blessed Sacrament, and I have remained faithful to it to this day.

For me adoration is a time of light and healing: In adoration, Jesus heals me by showing me how I hurt him. I welcome this light with joy because it allows me to undo an attitude that displeases his Father, by confessing my misery as soon as I am conscience of it. And each time it is a feast to be able to confess the mercy of God that heals me. In adoration, I give Jesus the only thing I fully possess: my unworthiness. In his eyes this has more value than my successes, which do not belong to me. "Your love makes me dance with joy: You see my misery and you know my adversity" (*Ps* 31:7 [Vulg.]).

Adoration, a time of offering, intercession, and spiritual motherhood: Offering my sufferings to the Father by uniting them to those of Christ for the redemption of sinners takes on all its meaning in adoration. For this reason, adoration made me understand that I had a real spiritual motherhood to exercise within the Church and that adoration was at the heart of evangelisation. The Father calls us all to be an offering – that is, to offer our everyday life, following Jesus, the first to have offered himself.

In Eucharistic adoration, then, one must offer one's person to Jesus. All the same, in the first place it is Jesus himself who remains in a permanent state of offering to his Father. His offering is made present in the tabernacle. The adorer, then, must enter into this offering. Jesus desires to let us share in his great offering to the Father. His whole life was a life of adoration and offering to the Father. Jesus leaves his great adoration of the Father to his Church in the tabernacle. In the Eucharist, he adores the Father and "always lives to make intercession for [us]" (*Heb* 7:25). In the Mystical Body, Jesus is the Head, and we the members. We must, then, enter into the same movement as the Head and unite ourselves to Jesus's permanent adoration of his Father, for "true worshippers will worship the Father in spirit and truth, for such the Father seeks to worship him" (*Jn* 4:23). Paul VI said: "And it is our very sweet duty to honour and adore in the blessed Host which our eyes see, the Incarnate Word whom they cannot see, and who, without leaving heaven, is made present before us."[6]

What does the Saviour do in the Eucharist? He continues his charge as adorer, as glorifier of his Father. He will make himself the Sacrament of God's glory. Do you see him, Jesus, on the altar? In the tabernacle? He is there; what is he doing there? He is adoring his Father, giving him thanks, and continuing his charge as the intercessor of men… He remains on his mystical Calvary repeating his sublime words: Father, forgive them! For them I offer you my blood, my wounds! He multiplies himself everywhere, everywhere where there is something to expiate. In whatever place that a Christian family establishes itself, Jesus comes to make a society of adoration with him and glorifies his Father by adoring him and making him to be adored in spirit and in truth. God the Father, satisfied, glorified as much as he deserves, cries out: "My name is great among the nations; for from the rising of the sun unto its setting, a host of pleasing fragrance is offered to me!"[7]

STAGE 3

"The Lord is my Shepherd"
The Evangelisation of my Being

> "I am the good shepherd. The good shepherd lays down his life for the sheep. He who is a hireling and not a shepherd, whose own the sheep are not, sees the wolf coming and leaves the sheep and flees; and the wolf snatches them and scatters them. He flees because he is a hireling and cares nothing for the sheep. I am the good shepherd; I know my own and my own know me, as the Father knows me and I know the Father; and I lay down my life for the sheep." (*Jn* 10:11-15)

See the table at the end of the chapter.

> "In giving you my presence in the tabernacle until the end of the centuries, I am giving you an infinite gift,… but I am giving you two other infinite gifts as well. In the second place, I am giving myself to you as your food, and in the third place, to be offered for you in sacrifice to my Father." (Bl. Charles de Foucauld)

The Lord is my shepherd, I shall not want; he makes me lie down in green pastures. He leads me beside still waters; he restores my soul. He leads me in paths of righteousness for his name's sake. Even though I walk through the valley of the shadow of death, I fear no evil; for you are with me; your rod and your staff, they comfort me. You prepare a table before me in the presence of my enemies; you anoint my head with oil, my cup overflows. Surely goodness and mercy shall follow me all the days of my life; and I shall dwell in the house of the Lord for ever. (*Ps* 23)

When the soul approaches the Eucharist with faith, Jesus acts towards it as a shepherd to his sheep. He leads it, feeds it, and heals it. In short, Jesus evangelises the whole interior being. For this, Jesus expects only that the soul have an interior predisposition that does not put up a barrier to the transformative power of Eucharistic grace.

a. Evangelisation of the body: "Adoration" (derived from the Latin "os": the mouth). Adoration includes a prostration whose goal is to attain and kiss the object of veneration. To adore, then, signifies: to bow profoundly in a sign of extreme respect. It is the natural attitude of man when he finds himself confronted with someone greater than himself. This posture is manifest throughout the book of Revelation: "The twenty-four elders fall down before him who is seated on the throne and worship him who lives for ever and ever; they cast their crowns before the throne" (*Rv* 4:10). Yes, we have the grace to know someone before whom we fall to our knees. The exterior posture conveys the interior devotion.

Etty Hillesum was a young Dutch Jewish woman. She was deported to Auschwitz, where she died in the last days of November 1943. A professor of Russian in Amsterdam, a refined intellectual, she found herself in the heart of the Nazi torment. When the atrocities against the Jews began, she too was arrested. From the camps where she stayed, Etty was able to write a few letters and a journal in each of which love always appears stronger than death. From the heart of suffering, she wrote: "My whole being is being transformed into a great prayer." Thomas of Celano reported this about Francis of Assisi: "Francis did not pray; he was prayer." In the midst of the hell of deportation, when the horror became unbearable, Etty left this last message: "I had the desire to kneel down on the tiles in the midst of all these people. The only gesture of human dignity that we still have in this terrible era: kneeling down before God."[8]

Bowing down to adore – this is man's ultimate goal.

b. Evangelisation of the gaze and of memory: Advertising campaigns unceasingly bombard our spirit with images, marked very often by sensuality, indeed, eroticism. Few major film productions are without any erotic or violent scenes. These images profoundly imprint themselves on the memory and harm our relationship with the Father. It takes years to be freed of this poison that pollutes the spirit and taints the heart. Jesus said: "Blessed are the pure in heart, for they shall see God" (*Mt* 5:8). In contemplating the Host, the resurrected Body of Christ, the Lord heals the heart, purifies the gaze, frees the unconscious from the most pernicious images, erases what is harmful from the memory, and renews the capacity to marvel at true beauty. Under the light of the Resurrected One, Christ touches our interior senses and chases away all darkness, because "the sun of righteousness shall rise, with healing in its wings" (*Ml* 4:2).

c. Evangelisation of the intellect: Let us enter into God's humility through the Eucharist. Faced with the incomprehensibility of the Eucharistic mystery, our intellect makes the words of Peter its own: "Lord, to whom shall we go? You have the words of eternal life; and we have believed, and have come to know, that you are the Holy One of God" (*Jn* 6:68-69). Since Jesus is the Truth, he cannot deceive us. He makes himself present in the Eucharist to enlighten our intellect. The *intellect* makes possible the study of theology, that is, the study of God. *Faith* pushes us to go before the Blessed Sacrament. One is the academic study of love, the other the sweet experience of Love embodied. At the end of her life, Pauline-Marie Jaricot wrote these poignant lines as her spiritual testament:

It is at the feet of your holy tabernacles that my heart, hardened by the harshest trials, has constantly found the strength necessary to endure their rigour; it is there that my struggles turned into victories, my weakness into courage, my lukewarmness into fervour, my uncertainties into lights, my sadness into joy, my obstacles into success, my desires into willpower, my dislikes, my jealousies, my resentments of my neighbour into ardent charity. All that I know, I have learned at your feet, Lord. Receive, then, the homage of all that I am, all that I have, all the good that I could ever think, say, and do.[9]

This is the homage of our intellect to the supreme divine intellect.

d. Evangelisation of the will: Let us enter into God's poverty. Although the universe cannot contain God, the Lord chooses to be contained bodily in a little Host, because love always tends to self-abasement beside the beloved person. To adore is to adhere, that is, freely to welcome God's will and his plan of love that unveils itself through Divine Providence. "Thy will be done" and not my own. Through adoration of the Blessed Sacrament, the Christian entirely gives back his own will to the Lord and lets God inspire his heart and put his supreme will in it. Adoration makes us enter into Jesus's prayer: "Abba, Father, all things are possible to you; remove this chalice from me; yet not what I will, but what you will" (*Mk* 14:36). The more faithful we are to God's will, the more our apostolic activity will be fruitful, for Jesus said: "Apart from me you can do nothing" (*Jn* 15:5).

Jesus is the Good Shepherd. We must learn to let ourselves be led and to abandon ourselves with confidence. Why should we not expect everything from him, for he said: "I myself will be the shepherd of my sheep, and I will make them lie down…I will seek the lost, and I will bring back the strayed, and I will bind up the crippled, and I will strengthen the weak" (*Ezk* 34:15-16). Our deepest wounds often prevent us from going towards others to serve them or announce the love of God to them. Jesus comes to heal these wounds when we approach the Eucharist with faith. He visits our heart and comes to fill it with his power and his healing love.

My Father, I abandon myself to you,
do with me what you will.
Whatever you do with me, I thank you.
I am ready for everything, I accept everything.
So long as your will is done in me,
in all your creatures,
I desire nothing else, my God.
I give back my soul into your hands.
I give it to you, my God,
with all the love of my heart,
because I love you,
and because for me it is a necessity of love to give myself,
to give myself back into your hands without measure,
with an infinite confidence,
for you are my Father.

Bl. Charles de Foucauld

What does a shepherd do for his sheep?	Jesus is the good shepherd (*Jn* 10)	Jesus in the Blessed Sacrament is our Shepherd
He feeds them.	"I came that they may have life, and have it abundantly" (*Jn* 10:10).	The Bread of Life strengthens the divine life in us (Holy Communion).
He leads them. He knows them, and they know his voice.	"If any one enters by me, he will be saved, and will go in and out and find pasture" (*Jn* 10:9). "I know my own and my own know me" (*Jn* 10:14).	In Eucharistic adoration, Jesus reveals himself to the heart. He lets himself be known. He leads and enlightens souls.
He protects them.	"I lay down my life for my sheep" (cf. *Jn* 10:11).	In the Holy Sacrifice of the Mass, Jesus offers himself as the spotless victim for the salvation of the world.

STAGE 4

"The Clay in the Potter's Hand"

"Like the clay in the potter's hand, so are you in my hand, O house of Israel" (*Jr* 18:6). We are the clay. God is the potter. God uses all of life's events to achieve the masterpiece he desires to accomplish in our souls. What is the masterpiece in question? "We know that in everything God works for good with those who love him… For those whom he foreknew he also predestined *to be conformed to the image of his Son*, in order that he might be the first-born among many brethren" (*Rm* 8:28-29).

> The witness of Scripture is unanimous that the solicitude of divine providence is *concrete* and *immediate*; God cares for all, from the least things to the great events of the world and its history. The sacred books powerfully affirm God's absolute sovereignty over the course of events: "Our God is in the heavens; he does whatever he pleases." [*Ps* 115:3] And so it is with Christ, "who opens and no one shall shut, who shuts and no one opens" [*Rv* 3:7]. As the book of Proverbs states: "Many are the plans in the mind of a man, but it is the purpose of the Lord that will be established" [*Pr* 19:21].[10]

Jesus demands a filial abandonment to the Providence of the heavenly Father, who cares for his children's least needs: "Therefore do not be anxious, saying, 'What shall we eat?' or 'What shall we drink?'… Your heavenly Father knows that you need [all these things]… But seek first his kingdom and his righteousness, and all these things shall be yours as well" (*Mt* 6:31-33; cf. 10:29-31). Jesus reminds us that the Divine Persons act unceasingly: "My Father is working still, and I am working" (*Jn* 5:17). The following verses make clear how God acts in the soul (*Jn* 15:2), for what end (*Jn* 15:8), and what our responses should be (*Jn* 15:4):

> I am the true vine, and my Father is the vinedresser. Every branch of mine that bears no fruit, he takes away, and every branch that does bear fruit he prunes, that it may bear more fruit. (*Jn* 15:1-2)

> Abide in me, and I in you. As the branch cannot bear fruit by itself, unless it abides in the vine, neither can you, unless you abide in me. (*Jn* 15:4)

> By this my Father is glorified, that you bear much fruit, and so prove to be my disciples. (*Jn* 15:8)

The verb "prune" evokes the work that God carries out in the soul of one who has begun to follow Jesus. To "abide in the vine" is to establish oneself in a communion of love with Jesus. This new life makes the faithful person able to bear "fruit". The vinedresser prunes the branches so that he may bear ever more fruit. It is the call to sanctity, the noblest and most beautiful adventure that a man can complete: "You shall be holy; for I the Lord your God am holy" (*Lv* 19:2).

Thus God uses all of life's events, the happy ones as well as the sad ones, to fortify us in his love and to reproduce the image of his Son in us. He desires to make of us "another Christ". It is often by the most dramatic events of life, like a personal failure, illness, or the loss of someone dear to us, that God prunes the soul by renewing our hope and our confidence in him. The greater our confidence, the greater will be the wonders worked in the soul by God: he uproots pride from our heart; he unbinds us from our self-satisfaction; he frees us from our attachments to the goods of this world. For this, Jesus left us Mary, one of whose titles is "Mother of Confidence". According to St Louis-Marie Grignon de Montfort, Mary is the "living mould of God" who reproduces her Son in us "without great pain or cost".

A sculptor has two ways of making a lifelike statue or figure: He may carve the figure out of some hard, shapeless material, using for this purpose his professional skill and knowledge, his strength and the necessary instruments, or he may cast it in a mould. The first manner is long and difficult and subject to many mishaps; a single blow of the hammer or the chisel, awkwardly given, may spoil the whole work. The second is short, easy and smooth;

it requires but little work and slight expense, provided the mould be perfect and made to reproduce the figure exactly; provided, moreover, the material used offer no resistance to the hand of the artist.

Mary is the great mould of God, made by the Holy Ghost to form a true God-Man by the Hypostatic Union and to form also a man-God by grace. In that mould none of the features of the Godhead is wanting. Whoever is cast in it, and allows himself be moulded, receives all the features of Jesus Christ, true God. The work is done gently, in a manner proportioned to human weakness, without much pain or labour, in a sure manner, free from all illusion… How many stains and defects and illusions, how much darkness and how much human nature is there in [the soul who trusts in its own skill and ingenuity]; and oh how pure, how heavenly and how Christ like is [the soul that is thoroughly tractable and casts itself into Mary to be moulded by the Holy Spirit].[11]

Adoration is a school of fervour in prayer. Whatever discipline we practise (physical, intellectual, or spiritual), regularity proves fundamental. No spiritual progress is possible without faithfulness in prayer. Without it, prayer would risk becoming sentimental: "I pray when I feel like it, or rather, if I have time after all my daily activities…" And our love for Jesus would come after everything else! Remember Jesus's words to Martha: "Martha, Martha, you are anxious and troubled about many things; one thing is needful. Mary has chosen the good portion, which shall not be taken away from her" (*Lk* 10:41-42). Mary was seated at Jesus's feet. For a moment, she leaves everything to belong entirely to Jesus. Through our regularity in prayer of adoration, we let God act in the soul, whatever the states of our souls! In parishes where continuous Eucharistic adoration is organised, the parishioners, who agree to commit themselves to a fixed hour of adoration every week, grow in faithfulness and attentiveness. Their commitment allows them not to be discouraged in moments of trial and spiritual dryness.

Also: a more limited commitment – for example, one hour of adoration per month – remains insufficient for letting this time of prayer transform us. Since Mass is a weekly commitment, and since adoration "prolongs and intensifies all that takes place during the liturgical celebration itself"[12] it makes sense to adore for an hour each week! As a practical matter, it is easier to free an hour per week than an hour per month since our schedules are established on a weekly basis.

Some state that they prefer to pray at home! Experience shows that it is more difficult to pray at home because of noise, distractions, or many inconveniences than in a chapel dedicated solely to silent prayer of adoration. The Eucharist is the sublime means that God, in the superabundance of his love, gives us so that man might unite himself to him.

The Church today strongly encourages the practice of Eucharistic adoration. It would be a shame to neglect it! To want to meet God in us in a "heart-to-heart" without passing through the "face to face" of adoration requires a purification of the inner self and a solid formation without which prayer risks leading us back to ourselves and not to God present in us. In the "face to face" of adoration, the resurrected Body of Jesus purifies us, transforms us, and divinises us. To contemplate the Host leads us to the "heart-to-heart" with Jesus and the Divine Persons.

A monstrance in barbed wire: Brother Claude Humbert, O.P., testifies about his stay at Dachau:

> Among the 4,000 priests who were at Dachau, a few had secretly fashioned a monstrance with barbed wire. For us, who were entirely surrounded with barbed wire, this monstrance took on an extraordinary meaning. It was Christ crowned with thorns and sharing our own. And the Body of Christ was often exposed in it. Like many priests, I spent long hours of adoration before him and Our Lady of Dachau at his right. This has marked me for life.[13]

STAGE 5

"Not What I Will, but What You Will"

And they went to a place which was called Gethsemane;
and he said to his disciples, "Sit here, while I pray." And he
took with him Peter and James and John, and began to be
greatly distressed and troubled. And he said to them, "My
soul is very sorrowful, even to death; remain here, and
watch." And going a little farther, he fell on the ground
and prayed that, if it were possible, the hour might pass
from him. And he said, "Abba, Father, all things are
possible to you; remove this chalice from me; yet not
what I will, but what you will." And he came and found
them sleeping, and he said to Peter, "Simon, are you
asleep? Could you not watch one hour? Watch and pray
that you may not enter into temptation; the spirit indeed
is willing, but the flesh is weak." And again he went away
and prayed, saying the same words. (*Mk* 14:32-39)

Scripture says that when Jesus was at Gethsemane, his "soul
was very sorrowful, even to death". He came to give his very
self to mankind through the gift of the Holy Eucharist. But
so many will reject this love! This rejection pierces his heart:
"I looked for pity, but there was none; and for comforters,
but I found none" (*Ps* 69:20). He called upon his apostles to
comfort him, but they preferred to sleep, for it was already

late at night. They slept during Christ's greatest agony, even after he had expressly called upon them: "So, could you not watch with me one hour?" (*Mt* 26:40). So, someone sent by the Father descended from heaven to console him. This angel comforted Jesus by showing him all our acts of love towards the Eucharist in the ages to come. Among other things, Jesus saw the numerous sacrifices of all those who would faithfully come to pray day and night, each week, to keep him company in the Blessed Sacrament. These sacrifices comforted, consoled, strengthened, and encouraged our Saviour. He knew then that his love would be requited, because "greater love has no man than this, that a man lay down his life for his friends" (*Jn* 15:13).

In Eucharistic adoration, the adorer learns to do no longer "his will for God", but "God's will". Every baptised person must live out this conversion of the will. Too often Christians generously exert themselves in many acts of service that they have chosen. At the end of the week, beyond physical fatigue, they experience a feeling of spiritual dissatisfaction, because they did their will for God. Jesus reminded us that the Father's will is true food: "My food is to do the will of him who sent me, and to accomplish his work" (*Jn* 4:34). Before acting, we must get on our knees, to receive from God not only his will, but also the strength to persevere in accomplishing it. Beyond this, prayer is a powerful defence against daily temptations: "Pray that you may not enter into temptation" (*Mk* 14:38).

"Abba, Father, all things are possible to you; remove this chalice from me; yet not what I will, but what you will" (*Mk* 14:36)! At Gethsemane, Jesus accepts the Father's will, even if it seems to be opposed to his personal will and leads him to the Cross. But it is in handing his life over to the Father that he saves mankind. Only the Father's will deserves to be done to the very end, for it gives man the means to bloom fully in his vocation as a child of the Father. Only the Father's will can truly fill man's heart by giving a profound meaning to life. All that we do outside of this will disappear irretrievably. Praying is not asking God to bless our own intentions, however good they may be. Praying is asking God for a new way of looking at the world, at others, and at oneself, as well as the grace to live in conformity to the divine will.

An adorer testifies: "At the beginning, I thought that adoration meant loving God greatly. But the Lord made me understand that he desires above all that I let myself be loved in my miseries and my faults. For me this is so much more demanding. Letting Jesus look at me, hold me, lead me to God his Father – that is adoration in spirit and in truth!"

Eucharistic adoration does not consist so much in "loving greatly" but rather in "letting oneself be greatly loved" despite our lacks and infidelities. In other words, it is not our qualities that attract Jesus but our faults. Eucharistic grace can then act through its transformative power. Let us allow Christ to continue in us the work of healing and sanctification that he began two thousand years ago. He comes not to receive our merits and virtues but to save and raise what is broken in our heart.

Eucharistic adoration makes us pass from "I" to "thou". It is inappropriate to begin by asking Jesus graciously to hear our will. Rather let us ask him to enlighten us about his will and to give us the grace to accomplish it. Adoration decentres us from ourselves in order to centre us on the person of Christ and on his holy will. Too often we pray like this: "Listen, Lord, for your servant speaks." Adoration drives us to say: "Speak, Lord, for your servant hears" (1 S 3:9).

In life today, often noisy and dispersive, it is more important than ever to recover the capacity for inner silence and recollection. Eucharistic adoration permits this not only centred on the "I" but more so in the company of that "You" full of love who is Jesus Christ, "the God who is near to us."[14]

Be faithful in abiding in God's presence without worrying about being unable to do anything... Do not be at all reluctant to be in God's presence without doing anything, for since he desires nothing from you but silence and annihilation, you will always be doing much when you leave and abandon yourself unreservedly to his omnipotence. Be faithful to this, do not be discouraged by your distractions, let them pass, and abide humbly at the feet of Jesus.[15]

Many saints' words about the ingratitude that Jesus receives in the Blessed Sacrament can be surprising. For example, Bl. Dina Bélanger, a religious in Quebec beatified by John Paul II, wrote:

> Oh! how harrowing are the plaints of Jesus! How he suffers, the silent Captive of our tabernacles, imprisoned day and night by love! So my greatest sorrow became that of the suffering of the Eucharistic Heart. How can one remain unmoved when it is Jesus who is abandoned and despised![16]

What are we to make of this?

It is true that since his Resurrection our Lord in the Host cannot suffer. But all the same, insult, contempt, hate, forgetfulness, indifference, and ingratitude reach and wound his Eucharistic Heart. Since his Resurrection, Christ enjoys a perfect beatitude. He is in no way a prisoner in tabernacles and not at all wounded by men's sins. However, when contemplative souls see our Lord suffering, even complaining to them about the sins and ingratitude of men, it is in no way an illusion. Jesus, in his sorrowful Passion, suffered from all the insults and all the ingratitude that were to be poured out upon him throughout the centuries, in his Sacrament of love. It is this suffering, and especially that proceeding from sins being committed at that moment, that he shares with his most faithful friends. So they have the impression that Jesus is suffering in the moment. They see, at that moment, Jesus such as he suffered in his agony, and they are called, then, to sympathise with his sufferings and to share them. It is thought that the angel who consoled our Lord in the garden on the Mount of Olives did so by showing him all the faithful souls who were to share in his sufferings until the end of the world. We can also say that our Lord suffers from men's offenses as the good God does (do we not say that sin gives sorrow to the good God), in the sense that he detests sin and that he acts towards it as if he were suffering from it. As Pope Pius XI explained in 1928, at Gethsemane, through "an angel who comforted him" (cf. *Lk* 22:43), Jesus, in his divine foreknowledge, foresaw our future efforts to console him and in his solitude that evening drew a real comfort from them.

STAGE 6

"Abba, Father"
Adoration: Remedy for Pride and Despair

Eucharistic adoration comes to heal man's heart. His heart is transformed into the heart of a child of God because the two great maladies of our time are pride and despair. Mankind's inordinate pride makes man believe that he can save himself all alone and that he can establish peace through science, technology, and the economy alone. And despair plunges our society into meaninglessness, into an interior decay. Pride consists in telling God that we have no need of him – no need of a Father. And despair does not know the Father; it makes us orphans. These two attitudes are sins against the virtue of hope. St Thomas Aquinas explains that the language of hope is the Our Father: "Abba, Father". To be healed from pride and despair we must say "Abba, Father". How can we live from the power of the Holy Spirit if this gift is not renewed in the Eucharist? Eucharistic adoration is a perpetual outpouring of the Holy Spirit to give us the heart of a child, to put us at the disposal of the Heart of God, to learn in those long hours spent before the Blessed Sacrament how to say "Abba, Father" with the right attitude: that is, in full charity, in the certitude that without him I can do nothing, and in acquiring the freedom of the children of God, which consists in being in perfect communion with the Father. Jesus came to do the will of the Father, to make the Father manifest.[17]

Man's natural path consists in separating from Dad and Mum in order to follow his own path. Spiritually, the path is just the opposite. So long as I do not depend upon the Father, I am a kid! But the more I enter into the heart of the Trinity, the more I become an adult in my humanity – in my humanity's spiritual dimension.

In respect to humanity, adoration's first fundamental healing is to give back a filial heart. The consequences affect not only us but also ecology. St Paul says:

> Creation waits with eager longing for the revealing of the sons of God; for the creation was subjected to futility, not of its own will but by the will of him who subjected it in hope; because the creation itself will be set free from its bondage to decay and obtain the glorious liberty of the children of God. We know that the whole creation has been groaning with labour pains together until now; and not only the creation, but we ourselves, who have the first fruits of the Spirit, groan inwardly as we wait for adoption as sons, the redemption of our bodies. (*Rm* 8:19-23)

One of the ways of interpreting this text is the following: creation suffers, groaning while waiting for men to behave as children of God, as sons of that heavenly Father who has given us creation as something in gestation and not as a possession to destroy. Thus today's ecological crisis concerning everything that must be done in order to avoid the tragedies that might occur has a profoundly spiritual root that we see explicitly here. Creation moans and groans in ecological catastrophes, waiting for man to behave as a child of God.

An Orthodox patriarch said: "Either the world will be transfigured by worship, or it will be disfigured by consumption." Here we touch upon that mysterious communion of all beings. Man is at the summit of creation and participates in all material nature through his physical nature. When man is no longer united to God, there is, as it were, a seismic tremor that radiates throughout the universe by the very fact that man's heart is no longer united to God. The first break happened through this disunity of mankind and God. To be attached to the Eucharistic Heart frees man, giving him the extraordinary freedom of the children of God. This freedom consists in living in charity, but without all of those subordinations into which we can fall. Adoration introduces us into that freedom of the children of God with all the consequences this implies for our daily behaviour.

Adoration is a duty of justice within the natural virtue of justice. We find it in the first gift of the Spirit, that of fear or adoration, which places us as creatures before the Creator in total adoration before him from whom all things come. This attitude of adoration is very important for our time. The world has lost its sense of adoration. It has lost its sense of kneeling. Man is great only on his knees, in adoration before God. A mankind that wants to remain standing, in its presumption, its pride, its self-satisfaction, that no longer knows how to kneel, has lost its sense of the essential. Going and kneeling before God interiorly, but also physically, is the fundamental attitude of the human heart. Eucharistic adoration comes to heal mankind from this secret wound rooted in original sin, which is the refusal to kneel before God, before him from whom all things come. On Christmas night 1886, Wagner wrote to Nietzsche about his searing spiritual experience. And Nietzsche responded: "What, ignoble man, you too have kneeled, you too have become a weakling, you too have prostrated yourself!" For the superman must not kneel. Mankind is caught in this myth of the superman and in his daily awareness of not being this superman. Adoration comes to break this structure of thought.

Adoration situates us in harmony. No power, no person, no thing, nothing is useless in creation; everything has its place in a spiritual symphony. Adoration is the revalorisation of every human being, of everything that is in us. Adoration is a transfiguration of the human being. A power of anthropological transformation acts through it. Fallen man is raised back up to the full stature of the dignity of a child of God. Personal adoration is also a place where the universe is transformed because it transforms man's heart. This is how God refashions the world. Adoration is the place where God reconstructs man.

Psychologically, our gaze fixes its attention on the Heart of Christ – the eyes of the flesh, but also the eyes of hope and charity, fixed on the Real Presence. There is no emotional excrescence in adoration! Rather it is peaceful and sometimes dry and arid. But this roots us in a deep distinction between what is of the emotional order and what comes from the faith at our very depths. This comes and profoundly heals what is wounded in us. "The sun of righteousness shall rise, with healing in its wings" (*Ml* 4:2). Adoration reconstructs man in his whole being, in an extremely profound way, even physically: he is there. Our body, our psychology, and our spiritual soul, with the intellect and the will, are transformed through the mystery of Eucharistic adoration. This transformation of the human person will be the key to the transformation of all mankind. The unity of the person will come through adoration.

Adoration urges us to action. We cannot stop where we are. After having contemplated Christ, King of glory, King of mankind, in the Blessed Sacrament, we must give forth actions, we must act. This Kingship must shine forth everywhere. "Faith is not the opiate of the people", said the economist François Perrou. "There is not a night I can go to sleep saying that I loved enough today." I will by lacking in love each time, be imploring God's grace to love more.

As St Peter Julian Eymard said so well:

> Exposition is the form of worship our time needs… It is necessary in order to save society. Society is killing itself, because it no longer has a centre of gravity and charity. There is no more family life: everyone isolates himself, concentrates on himself, wants to suffice unto himself. Disintegration is imminent. But society will be born again, full of vigour, when all its members come and join together around our Emmanuel. Spiritual relationships will be reformed quite naturally, under a common truth: the ties of true and strong friendship will be renewed under the action of just such a love… The great evil of the time is that we no longer go to Jesus Christ. We abandon the only foundation, the only law, the only saving grace… Returning to the source of life, to Jesus, and not only to Jesus passing through Judea or to Jesus glorified in heaven, but also and above all to Jesus in the Eucharist… Let us be quite clear, a century grows or declines in proportion to its worship of the divine Eucharist. This worship is the life and measure of its faith, its charity, and its virtue. May it come more and more, then, this Reign of the Eucharist.[18]

Your personal act of adoration assumes a cosmic and social dimension. It drives us towards action and gives rise to the transfiguration of the whole society. With the intellect's gaze, we would imagine at first sight that political and economic actions require great expertise, which is true. But with the gift of the intellect and of faith, we understand that if there is not this movement of adoration, this filial return of mankind to the Heart of God; if there is not this outpouring of the Holy Spirit, who brings together all of creation to the Father through mankind and who restores peace from the throne of mercy instituted by God on earth – his Blessed Sacrament – mankind cannot go forward. But if there is this movement, then we will see the most beautiful period of mankind shine forth before our eyes, the advent of the civilisation of love, this kingdom of peace and justice that will radiate through mankind in that nuclear fission of the Eucharist. And then there will be a historic Hosanna, a historic Palm Sunday when God is acclaimed King of kings upon the little donkey of the little Host.

SPIRITUAL WARFARE

STAGE 7

"Be Still, and Know that I Am God!"
Sensible Graces and Dryness

God is our refuge and strength, a very present help in trouble. Therefore we will not fear though the earth should change, though the mountains shake in the heart of the sea; though its waters roar and foam, though the mountains tremble with its tumult... The Lord of hosts is with us; the God of Jacob is our refuge. Come, behold the works of the Lord, how he has wrought desolations in the earth. He makes wars cease to the end of the earth; he breaks the bow, and shatters the spear, he burns the chariots with fire! "*Be still, and know that I am God. I am exalted among the nations, I am exalted in the earth!*" The Lord of hosts is with us; the God of Jacob is our refuge. (*Ps* 46:1-3, 7-11)

Going into a chapel of adoration or a church to spend some time before the Blessed Sacrament is learning how to be still! It is responding to the psalmist's invitation: "Be still, and know that I am God" (*Ps* 46:10). Jesus said: "Come away by yourselves to a lonely place, and rest a while" (*Mk* 6:31). Faced with daily stress and our overloaded lives, the need to be still becomes necessary. Physical strength can be renewed during a period of holiday. Spiritual strength can be renewed in a period of spiritual retreat or simply before the resurrected Christ who awaits us in the Blessed Sacrament!

During the day, St Thérèse of Lisieux would stop frequently to offer the world to God and to offer herself as a living host. Momentary fatigue often got the better of her. She writes:

> I should be desolate for having slept (for seven years) during my hours of prayer and my *thanksgivings* after Holy Communion; well, I am not desolate…I remember that *little children* are as pleasing to their parents when they are asleep as well as when they are wide awake; I remember, too, that when they perform operations, doctors put their patients to sleep. Finally, remember that "The Lord knows our weakness, that he is mindful that we are but dust and ashes."[19]

It is not what we do that makes a "holy hour", but what Jesus does: he pours into us his Holy Spirit, which sanctifies us. "If any one thirst, let him come to me and drink. He who believes in me, as the Scripture has said, 'Out of his heart shall flow rivers of living water'" (*Jn* 7:37-38). What counts above all for Jesus is our desire to love him. Instead of keeping an hour in our day free for our personal occupations, we choose to meet him in an hour of adoration.

Even if you think you cannot pray well because you are easily distracted, Jesus wants you to know that he understands this. It is natural. What he wants you to understand is supernatural: he loves you so much that the simple fact of choosing to spend an hour with him in prayer brings his Sacred Heart an indescribable joy!

And when we feel nothing or stop feeling anything? In adoration, what is most important is not what we feel but him whom we meet and what we give him! Love seeks, not its own interest, but the interest of the beloved. One does not go to worship for oneself or to feel something. We adore God for himself and because he deserves our adoration. Adoring is a "very sweet duty";[20] it is the first commandment: "You shall worship the Lord your God and him only shall you serve" (*Mt* 4:10).

One who states, "I no longer feel anything, so I'm going to stop adoration", has in fact never begun to adore! Prayer is never a question of feelings. For Jesus said, "true worshippers will worship the Father in spirit and truth, for such the Father seeks to worship him" (*Jn* 4:23), and not, "true worshippers will worship the Father in order to feel something, for such the Father seeks to worship him"!

Blessed be the God and Father of our Lord Jesus Christ, the Father of mercies and God of all comfort, who comforts us in all our afflictions, so that we may be able to comfort those who are in any affliction, with the comfort with which we ourselves are comforted by God. For as we share abundantly in Christ's sufferings, so through Christ we share abundantly in comfort too. (*2 Cor* 1:3-5)

During times of adoration, Jesus can give the soul, in a limited way, very sensible graces. He gives us the consolations appropriate to our situation and according to our needs. But during his prayer, the adorer ought never to seek these graces for themselves. Sensible graces are transitory. Graces that build up the interior life are lasting and fortify divine union. Too often adorers feel discouraged when adoration becomes arid, because of their excessive attraction to the sensible consolations that they have stopped receiving. The Lord purifies the adorer's faith. He prunes the soul according to these words: "Every branch that does bear fruit [my Father] prunes, that it may bear more fruit" (*Jn* 15:2). The Father always lavishes us with his graces. They become less sensible but act more profoundly in the soul and bear more abundant fruit. The soul then passes from a sensible attachment to God to an adoration of God in spirit and truth.

Content yourself, not with what you are, not with what you feel, but with what God is and what he will be for ever... The rest is not worth thinking about. Only worry about God. All the rest is nothing. So the soul knows one thing, which is that God is, and it is there she stops, no longer amused with watching or reflecting upon all that is happening inside of her or outside of her. Paying no attention to all that, she abides always in God.[21]

And distractions?

It is with the heart that we pray, and a sincere and persevering will to pray is a true prayer. Distractions that are entirely involuntary do not interrupt the bending of the will towards God... Do not attack distractions directly: to protest against the distraction itself is to be distracted... You would spend all your time warring against the flies making noise around you: let them drone in your ears, and accustom yourself to continuing your journey as if they were far from you. Take hold of the places in the Gospel that touch you most. Read slowly, and when some word touches you, let this truth drip little by little into your heart.[22]

In the midst of distractions, we can also change our bodily position by, for example, getting back on our knees for a few minutes. We can also choose another way of praying, like meditating on the Rosary, on the Gospel, or reading a passage from a devotional book.

Why do so many distractions monopolise us? Throughout the day, preoccupations, meetings, and worries so solicit the spirit that it makes sense that it needs time to calm down. This is why many distractions often assail the spirit during the first part of an hour's adoration. Afterwards, the imagination is less of a disruption and the spirit is less active. It is often then that the heart is receptive to divine inspirations and that prayer of adoration becomes a real heart-to-heart. This also explains why night-time adoration is much more conducive to recollection, because the day's activities solicit the spirit less.

To overcome dryness and spiritual droughts, committing to an hour of adoration per week is strongly recommended. Some people refuse to choose a specific hour, preferring to come "freely", according to their pleasure. A deceptive desire and a dangerous fidelity! Love drives us to commitment. Freedom is fully exercised when it is committed to fidelity in love. To overcome an affective adoration (adoring when one feels like it, going to see "one's own little Jesus") and move on to an adoration "in spirit and truth", an adoration in the Church and for the Church, it is necessary to pray faithfully and regularly! Adoration then becomes a service for mankind. We keep watch in the name of the Church for those most in need of it. Experience shows that commitment to a fixed hour allows us to persevere through dry periods and spiritual droughts.

48

STAGE 8

Jacob's Struggle and Spiritual Advice

Jacob was left alone; and a man wrestled with him until the breaking of the day. When the man saw that he did not prevail against Jacob, he touched the hollow of his thigh; and Jacob's thigh was put out of joint as he wrestled with him. Then he said, "Let me go, for the day is breaking." But Jacob said, "I will not let you go, unless you bless me." And he said to him, "What is your name?" And he said, "Jacob." Then he said, "Your name shall no more be called Jacob, but Israel, for you have striven with God and with men, and have prevailed." Then Jacob asked him, "Tell me, I pray, your name." But he said, "Why is it that you ask my name?" And there he blessed him. So Jacob called the name of the place Peniel, saying, "For I have seen God face to face, and yet my life is preserved." (*Gn* 32:24-30)

Note from the Jerusalem Bible:

This enigmatic story…speaks of a physical struggle, a wrestling with God from which Jacob seems to emerge victor. Jacob recognises the supernatural character of his adversary and extorts a blessing from him. The text, however, avoids using the name of Yahweh and the unknown antagonist will not give his name. The author has made use of an old story as a means of explaining the name "Peniel" ("face of God") and the origin of the name "Israel". At the same time he gives the story a religious significance: the patriarch holds fast to God and forces from him a blessing: henceforth all who bear Israel's name will have a claim on God. It is not surprising that this dramatic scene later served as an image of the spiritual combat and of the value of persevering prayer (St Jerome, Origen).

Humble yourselves therefore under the mighty hand of God, that in due time he may exalt you. Cast all your anxieties on him, for he cares about you. Be sober, be watchful. Your adversary the devil prowls around like a roaring lion, seeking someone to devour. Resist him, firm in your faith, knowing that the same experience of suffering is required of your brotherhood throughout the world. And after you have suffered a little while, the God of all grace, who has called you to his eternal glory in Christ, will himself restore, establish, and strengthen you. (*1 P* 5:6-10)

In this passage, the apostle Peter invites us to enter into the spiritual battle of prayer. It is a battle greater than we are, for which God remains our only help:

Put on the whole armour of God, that you may be able to stand against the wiles of the devil. For we are not contending against flesh and blood, but against the principalities, against the powers, against the world rulers of this present darkness, against the spiritual hosts of wickedness in the heavenly places (*Ep* 6:11-12).

The devil will do anything to keep us from praying. Activism will always be a temptation not to pray any more. Even works that are good in themselves can become pretexts to stop praying or to not pray at all. God himself must always come before works for God. In prayer, the Spirit comes to fight in us against the spirit of the world and to make us say: "Abba, Father".

For all who are led by the Spirit of God are sons of God. For you did not receive the spirit of slavery to fall back into fear, but you have received the spirit of sonship. When we cry, "Abba, Father!" it is the Spirit himself bearing witness with our spirit that we are children of God (*Rm* 8:14-16).

This warfare is not simply against the demon; first of all it is against ourselves, against our sin. Praying is hard, not only for us, but for the "brotherhood throughout the world". Everyone who is baptised must participate in the same warfare, with the same temptations and the same difficulties. For each victory in faithfulness and perseverance, God rewards us by strengthening our communion with him.

He will "restore, establish, and strengthen you" (*1 P* 5:10). Hence the importance of committing to a weekly hour of adoration in order to be supported by the community and persevere to the end!

Let us be "soldiers for peace"! Through the centuries, innumerable men have sacrificed their lives during wars. Today, so few are ready to make the least sacrifice to win peace. Evil wins in our world today because those against God are more active than those for God. This spiritual warfare between good and evil is taking place today. It is the greatest war in human history because the destiny of the Church and the world depends on it. It is a spiritual "red alert". Who will react against general indifference and become a courageous soldier for Christ, fighting for peace through prayer? Who will become a man of God, arming himself with the spiritual arms of prayer and self-renunciation? "For God did not give us a spirit of timidity but a spirit of power and love and self-control" (*2 Tm* 1:7). Who will respond to Christ's call launched in the middle of the night: "Simon, are you asleep? Could you not watch one hour?" (*Mk* 14:37).

Some advice on how to spend an hour with Jesus
in the Blessed Sacrament

Is there a universal method for adoring the Blessed Sacrament? No, because adoration has us enter into a relationship of love. And in love, there can be no rules or laws. It is a heart that meets another heart in perfect freedom. "Man's humility is needed in order to respond to God's humility."[23] Time, silence, and patience are required. All the saints knew how to let the Holy Spirit lead them in this intimate relationship with Christ. Jesus awaits us in the sacrament of his Love. Praying an hour in the presence of Jesus is not hard, because Jesus is without doubt the easiest person to meet. We can help ourselves with a prayer book, passages of Scripture, or the Rosary. Better yet, know how to enter into interior silence by speaking heart-to-heart with Jesus as with a friend. More than anything, the Lord desires our heart. He desires to speak with us, bless us, sanctify us, take hold of us, and lead us to his Father. It may happen that we are so tired and weak that we do not want to do anything but sit and rest to feel the sweet peace that comes from the simple fact of being in the presence of him who loves us most, Jesus in the Blessed Sacrament, who says: "Come to me, all who labour and are heavy laden, and I will give you rest" (*Mt* 11:28). "My peace I give to you" (*Jn* 14:27).

Adoring with Holy Scripture: "If you read the Gospel, bring it to the Eucharist, and from the Eucharist into yourself. You then have a much greater power. The Gospel becomes clear, and you have before your eyes and in reality the continuation of what you are reading"[24].

Adoring with the Rosary: when you pray the Rosary in the presence of the Blessed Sacrament, you love Jesus with the heart of Mary. You offer Jesus Mary's perfect adoration. Jesus welcomes your hour of adoration as if it came from Mary herself. Mary receives you into her heart, and Jesus accepts your hour spent with him as if it came directly from the heart of his most blessed Mother. Mary's heart fills the deficiencies in our own heart. "The Rosary itself, when it is profoundly understood in the biblical and Christocentric form…, will prove a particularly fitting introduction to Eucharistic contemplation, a contemplation carried out with Mary as our companion and guide."[25]

Mother Teresa wrote:

I do an hour of adoration every day in the presence of Jesus in the Blessed Sacrament. All my Missionary Sisters of Charity also do their hour of adoration. For us, thanks to this daily hour of adoration, our love for Jesus becomes more intimate, our love for each other more meaningful, and our love for the poor more compassionate. Our daily hour of adoration is our family prayer when we come together before the Blessed Sacrament exposed in the monstrance. For the first half hour, we recite the Rosary, and for the second half hour we pray in silence. Through our adoration, the number of our vocations has doubled. In 1963, we did one hour of adoration together each week, but it was only in 1973, when we began doing our daily hour of adoration, that our community began to grow and prosper.[26]

The Holy Sacrifice of the Mass is the most sublime of prayers. In it, Jesus Christ offers himself to his Father, adores him, thanks him, asks his forgiveness, and implores him for the good of his Church, for sinful men. Jesus continues this majestic prayer through his state of victimhood in the Eucharist. St Peter Julian Eymard suggests dividing the hour of adoration into four periods, corresponding to the four ends of the sacrifice of the Mass, namely: adoration, thanksgiving, reparation, and supplication. Here are a few of the saint's words:

Adoration: If you begin with love, you will end with love. Offer Christ your person, your actions, your life. Adore the Father through the Eucharistic Heart of Jesus. He is God and man, your Saviour and your brother at once. Adore the heavenly Father through his Son, the object of all his kindness, and your adoration will be worth Jesus's adoration: it will be his adoration.

Thanksgiving: Thanksgiving is the act of love that is sweetest to the soul and most pleasing to God; it is the perfect homage to his infinite goodness. The Eucharist itself is the perfect act of gratitude. Eucharist means *thanksgiving*: in it Jesus gives thanks to his Father for us. In it he is our own thanksgiving. Thank the Father, the Son, and the Holy Spirit for giving us the gift of the Eucharist.

Reparation: for all the sins against his Eucharistic presence. What sadness for Jesus to remain ignored, abandoned, despised in so many tabernacles! How few Christians believe in his Real Presence, how many forget him, all this because he made himself so very small, so very humble in order to show us his love! Ask forgiveness, make the mercy of God descend upon the world for all crimes.

Intercession, supplication: Pray that his kingdom come, that men believe in his Eucharistic presence. Pray for the world's intentions, for your own intentions. And end your adoration with acts of love and adoration.[27]

56

STAGE 9

The Trial in the Wilderness
Adoration in Battle, Recollection, Contemplation

The Israelites wandered through the wilderness for forty years before arriving in the Promised Land. This symbolises our faithful progress in faith until the day when we see God face to face. In the wilderness, the Israelites sometimes had the experience of desolation and sometimes were filled with divine favours. In fact, the word "wilderness" in Hebrew signifies the place of "desolation" where one abandons God or, conversely, the place of the "Word" where one seeks him with all one's heart. It is in the wilderness that God addressed his people at Sinai, there that he gave the tablets of the Law, there that he made a covenant with them, there that he chose them as his bride. It is there that he desired to bring back his unfaithful people to recover the abandoned Covenant: "Therefore, behold, I will allure her, and bring her into the wilderness, and speak tenderly to her… And I will espouse you for ever; I will espouse you in righteousness and in justice, in steadfast love, and in mercy" (*Ho* 2:14, 19). The permanent presence of the Host in each church reveals God's unceasing faithfulness towards us. Contemplating the Host is choosing God anew; it is allowing oneself to be looked at, called, and espoused anew!

Each year, the Church offers periods of grace, like that of Lent, to renew our covenant with God – a covenant sealed in the Eucharist. When worldly cares have taken the upper hand, God can send us into the wilderness in order to recover the love we had at the beginning:

> I know you are enduring patiently and bearing up for my name's sake, and you have not grown weary. But I have this against you, that you have abandoned the love you had first. Remember then from what you have fallen, repent and do the works you did at first (*Rv* 2:3-5).

When the Lord leads us into the wilderness, we feel the dryness, the drought. So it is the place of adoration: we adore; it is hard; we must dig, dig. This depends on us. But this difficult and tiring step requires a great deal of willpower, effort, perseverance. It is the time of "*adoration in battle*"[28] so valuable to the soul because God is strengthening its faith. Adoration in the wilderness requires a great deal of willingness! So we must beg the Holy Spirit to strengthen in us the "gift of fortitude" so as never to be discouraged. We must strengthen our will by digging ever deeper so as never to remain in places where there is no more water.

> You are in dryness, glorify the grace of God, without which you can do nothing; open your soul to heaven, then, as the flower opens its calix at the rising of the sun to receive the life-giving dew.[29] You are in a state of total powerlessness, the spirit is in darkness, the

heart under the weight of its nothingness, the body suffering, so practise the adoration of the poor man. Leave your poverty and go abide in our Lord, or offer him your poverty so that he may enrich it. This is a masterpiece worthy of his glory. But you are in the state of temptation and sorrow; everything in you revolts; everything prompts you to stop adoring on the pretext that you are offending God, that you are dishonouring him more than you are serving him; do not listen to this specious temptation, this is adoration in battle, adoration faithful to Jesus against yourself. No, no, you are not displeasing him; you are giving joy to your Master at whom you are looking. He expects from us the homage of perseverance until the last minute of time that we are to devote to him.[30]

Faced with our efforts in adoration, the Holy Spirit always gives a little dew, a little love that makes us pass from adoration in battle against ourselves to a life-giving adoration or a *recollective adoration*. "The labourer deserves his wages" (*Lk* 10:7). The Spirit transforms everything according to the prophecy of Ezekiel: "I will give them one heart, and put a new spirit within them; I will take the stony heart out of their flesh and give them a heart of flesh" (*Ezk* 11:19). This is what Jesus revealed to St Faustina:

While I was at the church, to confess, I perceived these same rays (those represented on the divine mercy image) coming forth from the monstrance. They spread throughout the whole church. This lasted the whole length of the office. After benediction, they spread from the two sides, then came back to the monstrance. They looked clear and transparent like crystal. I prayed to Jesus that he might deign to light the fire of his love in all cold souls. Under these rays, their heart would warm, even if it was cold as ice, and it would be reduced to dust, even if it was as hard as rock.[31]

But the Holy Spirit does not want us to think of this grace as something owed to us. We must not stop digging; rather, we must continue to seek this love with our will, always deeper, relentlessly. Sometimes the Holy Spirit carries us in such a way that we can no longer dig. Then we must let him do so. This happens regularly to some souls that are advanced in the interior life. The Spirit leads us to a true intimacy with the Heart of Christ. God then gives *contemplative graces* of light, of presence. This is an anticipation of the beatific vision. This is the Spirit who wants us already to participate, despite the darkness of faith, in the face-to-face encounter that awaits us in heaven, with God, Mary, the saints, the angels. Through contemplation, love becomes so strong that the presence exceeds anything that we could see. This presence changes our way of looking at the world and at others. It pushes us to action. So we should let the Spirit lead us into the wilderness!

Here are a few reflections on the value of night-time adoration:

Language of love: A father and mother must make many sacrifices to feed, shelter, and educate their children. Without sacrifice, there is no love. The spirit of sacrifice is the spirit of the Christian. Through love Jesus sacrificed everything for us and our salvation. Through love of him, will we agree to offer one hour at night each week with him, in adoration of the Blessed Sacrament, so that our parish might have perpetual Eucharistic adoration?

God abundantly blesses us: The holy Eucharist is the sacrament of God's infinite generosity towards men. By our generous response to this sacrament of Love, God pours his infinite goodness on mankind. God will greatly bless you, your family, and the whole world for this precious gift of your time, because God never allows himself to be outdone in generosity. Whatever we may give to him, he gives us back tenfold or a hundredfold. Those who generously accept to make the effort of choosing one of the most difficult hours of the night bring down divine blessings upon earth, like rain falling from heaven. This is why John Paul II affirmed: "Let us be generous with our time in going to meet Him in adoration."[32]

Our act of faith will make the streets safer! Through his prophets Haggai and Zechariah, God declares that the dangers of the streets will disappear for his people when they seek the glory of the sanctuary. Those who agree to visit Jesus in the middle of the night are those seeking the glory of his sanctuary. It is they who release God's power, thus bringing safety into the streets. In uniting ourselves to Jesus in the Blessed Sacrament, we unite ourselves to the all-powerfulness of the Resurrected One. When we go before Jesus in the Blessed Sacrament, we release his power and his graces for the whole world. This is why Jesus said: "If you had faith as a grain of mustard seed, you could say to this sycamine tree, 'Be rooted up, and be planted in the sea,' and it would obey you" (*Lk* 17:6). Those who agree to make the sacrifice of coming to Jesus in the middle of the night have this faith! They put their faith in the greatest power on earth. This explains why the rate of crime diminishes in the vicinity of a church where perpetual adoration has been instituted!

We make reparation for the world's great errors: Evil must be vanquished by good. The greatest evil must be vanquished by the greatest good. The extraordinary evil of our society must be vanquished by the extraordinary good of perpetual adoration of Jesus in the Blessed Sacrament. The sacrifice of spending an hour in the middle of the night each week will drive away evil from our land, turning the waterworks of merciful love upon mankind. This is why Pope John Paul II, in calling for "adoration never [to] cease", asks us to be "ready to make reparation for the great faults and crimes of the world".[33]

STAGE 10

The Power of Intercession
Moses Fights against the Amalekites
The Paralytic

Then came Amalek and fought with Israel at Rephidim.
And Moses said to Joshua, "Choose for us men, and go
out, fight with Amalek; tomorrow I will stand on the top
of the hill with the rod of God in my hand." So Joshua
did as Moses told him, and fought with Amalek; and
Moses, Aaron, and Hur went up to the top of the hill.
Whenever Moses held up his hand, Israel prevailed; and
whenever he lowered his hand, Amalek prevailed. But
Moses's hands grew weary; so they took a stone and put
it under him, and he sat upon it, and Aaron and Hur
held up his hands, one on one side, and the other on
the other side; so his hands were steady until the going
down of the sun. And Joshua mowed down Amalek and
his people with the edge of the sword. (*Ex* 17:8-13)

Moses was the great intercessor between God and Israel.
Yet in this passage, Moses could not sufficiently intercede
on his own strength. He needed to ask for help from Hur,
the commander of his army, and from his brother, Aaron.
The two supported Moses's arms raised up towards God.
Thus, Moses's intercession became unceasing. And God

gave his people total victory against their enemies. It is the same with perpetual adoration. Parishioners arrange their schedules together, one after another, forming an uninterrupted chain of prayer and intercession in such a way that the heart of the parishioners is turned unceasingly towards God. And God also gives his people total victory by abundantly pouring forth his light, which drives away shadows, and his mercy, which warms hearts.

This is the power of the intercessory prayer of a Christian community that prays day and night at the feet of the Lord. The spiritual benefits of such a prayer are not primarily personal but above all communal.

The more the earth comes into alignment with itself by perpetually adoring God, the more the kingdom of God descends upon earth with its peace, light, and Spirit.

Isaiah prophesied about the New Jerusalem that prefigures the Church:

> You shall no more be termed Forsaken, and your land shall no more be termed Desolate; but you shall be called My delight is in her, and your land Married; for the Lord delights in you, and your land shall be married. For as a young man marries a virgin, so shall your sons marry you, and as the bridegroom rejoices over the bride, so shall your God rejoice over you. Upon your walls, O Jerusalem, I have set watchmen; all the day and all the night they shall never be silent. (*Is* 62:4-6)

When a parish organises perpetual adoration, the "watchmen" are the adorers on the "walls" who are "never silent". In other words, through their unceasing prayer, they are held up between heaven and earth and bring down upon mankind the waterworks of divine mercy. The adorer enters into Christ's unceasing intercession of his Father at the tabernacle. The adorer is put on the fractures of mankind. His supplication embraces all situations where man has lost his dignity, his wholeness, his resemblance to the Father. Adoration evangelises by pouring forth the graces of redemption through the Church on all situations where man no longer responds to his vocation as a child of God.

Thus, through Eucharistic adoration, we do a great service for mankind.

Through adoration, the Christian contributes to the radical transformation of the world. Every person who prays to the Lord brings the whole world along with him, raising the world to God. Thus those who remain before the Lord fulfil a great service.[34]

Isaiah also prophesies that the New Jerusalem will be the perfect bride of the divine Bridegroom. Perpetual adoration is the love song of the Church-Bride to her Bridegroom who gives himself in the Eucharist. "Come, Lord Jesus!" (*Rv* 22:20) for the eternal nuptials, first with the soul, but one day with all of mankind. In giving the Lord the honour and glory that are due to his name through perpetual adoration, we proclaim Jesus King of love and mercy. We pray unceasingly that he take possession of his kingdom (*Rv* 11:17; 19:6), while waiting for him to realise his promise: "Behold, I make all things new" (*Rv* 21:5) because "according to his promise we wait for new heavens and a new earth in which righteousness dwells" (*2 P* 3:13).

Finally, through unceasing adoration, the light of the Resurrected One drives away the shadows from the world and makes present in our lives his victory on the Cross. As the Lord gave victory to his people by destroying the walls of Jericho after having encircled them seven times, likewise the Lord gives it to us to vanquish all our Jerichos, whether they be evil itself or our personal failings, when we perpetually adore him in the Blessed Sacrament. "By faith the walls of Jericho fell down after they had been encircled for seven days" (*Heb* 11:30). Since seven represents fullness, when the people of God remain day and night in faith before the Blessed Sacrament, the Lord works the miracles that the Church and mankind need.

> When he returned to Capernaum after some days, it was reported that he was at home. And many were gathered together, so that there was no longer room for them, not even about the door; and he was preaching the word to them. And they came, bringing to him a paralytic carried by four men. And when they could not get near him because of the crowd, they removed the roof above

him; and when they had made an opening, they let down the pallet on which the paralytic lay. And when Jesus saw their faith, he said to the paralytic, "Child, your sins are forgiven." (*Mk* 2:1-5)

Jesus is teaching in Peter's house at Capernaum. The masses crowd around him to hear him. The paralytic's four friends are not discouraged by the apparent impossibility of presenting the sick man to Jesus. They give evidence of daring, perseverance, determination. Seeing their faith, Jesus says: Your sins are forgiven. Nothing is said about the faith of the paralytic. Maybe he asked to be presented to Jesus, maybe not. What is certain is that Jesus lets himself be moved by the faith of the four men. It is their persevering faith that pushes Jesus to forgive sins. It is not said, "when Jesus saw his faith", but "when Jesus saw their faith".

In the same way, when we are at the foot of the Blessed Sacrament, we can present to Jesus those close to us, our friends, the members of our family, or simply the whole world. Then Jesus likewise says: "Your sins are forgiven." Through intercessory prayer, Jesus gives the graces to return to God the Father to those for whom we intercede. Through our faith in adoration, we touch the Heart of Jesus, which touches the Heart of God. In return, God touches all the hearts of mankind.

Here are some words by St Maximilian Kolbe, a Polish priest who died at Auschwitz by freely taking the place of a man condemned to death: "Prayer is a poorly known means, and yet the most effective, for establishing peace in souls, for giving them happiness, since it serves to bring them closer to the love of God."[35]

The most important activity, namely, prayer, is in the midst of development. To the practices we had before has been added perpetual adoration of the Most Blessed Sacrament. At first two brothers taking turns, then four, and now six brothers take half-hour turns all day long; and thus a torrent of prayer flows uninterruptedly throughout the whole day, the greatest power of the universe, capable of transforming us and changing the face of the world.[36]

"The value of each member of Niepokalanów depends only and exclusively on his prayer life, on his interior life, on our personal coming closer to the Immaculate and, through her, to the Heart of Jesus."[37]

68

STAGE 11

"A Prophet is without Honour
in His Own Country"
Welcoming the Saviour

He went away from there and came to his own country;
and his disciples followed him. And on the Sabbath he
began to teach in the synagogue; and many who heard
him were astonished, saying, "Where did this man get
all this? What is the wisdom given to him? What mighty
works are wrought by his hands! Is not this the carpenter,
the son of Mary and brother of James and Joseph and
Judas and Simon, and are not his sisters here with us?"
And they took offense at him. And Jesus said to them,
"A prophet is not without honour, except in his own
country, and among his own kin, and in his own house."
And he could not do mighty work there, except that he
laid his hands upon a few sick people and healed them.
And he marvelled because of their unbelief. (*Mk* 6:1-6)

Jesus comes to Nazareth, his hometown. He comes to
announce the Good News of the kingdom of God. He
hopes to work the miracles he has accomplished elsewhere
in his own home. But because of the unbelief of the
inhabitants, "he could not do mighty work there." What
pathos to see Jesus sorrowfully retain the graces coming

from the Father in his Heart because of their unbelief. Yes, faith is the key that opens the Heart of Jesus and sets free his power, his healing love, his divine life, and the glory of his Resurrection. Without man's response, God can do nothing in the soul. God infinitely respects human freedom. But his greatest desire is to find open hearts that await everything from him.

"A prophet is not without honour, except in his own country." Too often what so sadly happened at Nazareth continues in the Church. Jesus is present today among his own, his country, in the heart of each church. In the tabernacle, Christ is present in person with his body, blood, soul, and divinity. He is there, his hands filled with spiritual treasures that he wishes to pour forth abundantly upon his children. Unfortunately, our churches are so often closed, deserted. Today in the tabernacle, as yesterday at Nazareth, Jesus is ignored, misunderstood, and cannot "do mighty work" because of our unbelief!

Along these lines, St Peter Julian Eymard implored: "Do not leave hosts sterile!"[38] We should of course understand that there is no sterility possible in the Eucharist, because it is the Sacrament of divine fruitfulness that gives us divine life and makes us supportive of one another: "I am the vine, you are the branches. He who abides in me, and I in him, he it is that bears much fruit, for apart from me you can do nothing" (*Jn* 15:5). All the same, if we do not have faith, Jesus cannot grant his graces and renew his mighty works in our hearts. Let us pray that our Christian communities never experience this tragic episode from Nazareth. May all our pastoral activities find their source and centre in the tabernacle, "the living heart of each of our churches".[39]

In many places, *adoration of the Blessed Sacrament* is also an important daily practice and becomes an inexhaustible source of holiness... Unfortunately, alongside these lights, *there are also shadows*. In some places the practice of Eucharistic adoration has been almost completely abandoned.[40]

By recognising him today under the appearances of bread, Jesus calls us blessed, as he said to Thomas: "You have believed because you have seen me. Blessed are those who have not seen and yet believe" (*Jn* 20:29). Blessed the soul that knows how to find Jesus in the Eucharist and all things in Jesus!

Bl. Dina Bélanger of Quebec wrote:

If souls understood what a treasure they possessed in the divine Eucharist, it would be necessary to protect tabernacles with impregnable walls; for, in the delirium of a holy and devouring hunger, they would go themselves to be nourished by the Manna of the Seraphim. Churches, at night as during the day, would overflow with adorers consumed by love for the noble prisoner.[41]

When he drew near and saw the city he wept over it, saying, "Would that even today you knew the things that make for peace! But now they are hidden from your eyes. For the days shall come upon you, when your enemies will cast up a bank about you and surround you, and hem you in on every side, and dash you to the ground, you and your children within you, and they will not leave one stone upon another in you; because you did not know the time of your visitation." (*Lk* 19:41-44)

Here, Jesus weeps over Jerusalem. Just as the inhabitants of Nazareth had not understood Jesus's divine origin and mission, so too Jerusalem does not recognise the Lord and the peace that he comes bearing from his Father. The act of faith made in order to recognise Jesus two thousand years ago is the same act that must be made today in order to recognise him in the Eucharist. His mission is to bear peace, "for he is our peace" (*Ep* 2:14). Jesus said to St Faustina, "Mankind will not find Peace so long as it does not turn with confidence to my Mercy."[42] "The throne of Mercy is the Tabernacle."[43] Thus, there cannot be true peace in hearts, in families, and in the world without turning entirely to the tabernacle, to the Eucharist.

Here is the circumstance in which Mother Mechtilde was inspired to found the institute of Perpetual Adoration. Finding herself at the home of Madame de Boves, she:

saw there a painting representing a pagan ceremony, where priests and priestesses worshipped an idol, holding a flame in their hands, and vestal virgins looked after the sacred fire. Gripped by a profound emotion in the presence of this canvas, the venerable Mother could not keep herself from saying to the marchioness: "Madame, the idolaters will one day be our damnation and that of Christians who have so little respect for the Most Blessed Sacrament in churches. What we do not do for our God that these pagans did for their false gods! Why, in his house where he continually dwells, should he not be continually adored? Why should not the sentinels of Israel watch day and night, never growing tired, around the throne of the Solomon of the New Law?"[44]

The mission of the adorer's prayer is eminently apostolic. Although it seems that nothing is happening, everything is happening before the Blessed Sacrament. John Paul II reminded us:

In the Holy Eucharist – this is also the meaning of perpetual adoration – we enter into the movement of love from which all interior progress and all apostolic fruitfulness flows: "I, when I am lifted up from the earth, will draw all men to myself" (*Jn* 12:32).[45]

By exposing him and uniting ourselves to his prayer and apostolate through our adoration, we make our Lord work for the conversion of souls. This is the special privilege of our calling to expose our Lord and put him in the solemn exercise of his role as mediator. *Indeed, it is only because we are at his feet that he is on his throne.* The Church would not allow him to perpetuate his presence day and night if he were not to find adorers following one after another in order to serve him day and night: to make himself manifest in his exposition, we are necessary for him; we release his power.[46]

Now, we must quickly get to work, saving souls through the divine Eucharist and awakening France and Europe, numbed in its sleep of indifference because it does not know God's gift, Jesus the Eucharistic Emmanuel. It is the flame of love that we must carry into tepid souls that think themselves pious and are not, because they have not established their centre and life in Jesus in the Holy Tabernacle; and every devotion that does not have a tent on Calvary and one around the tabernacle is not a solid piety and will never amount to much. We distance ourselves too much from the Holy Eucharist; we do not preach often enough about this mystery of love par excellence; so souls suffer, they become entirely sensual and material in their piety, inordinately attaching themselves to creatures, because they do not know how to find their consolation and strength in our Lord.[47]

74

Endnotes

[1] John Paul II, Encyclical Letter *Ecclesia de Eucharistia* (2003), no. 61.

[2] St Peter Julian Eymard, *Adorer en Esprit et en Vérité* (Paris: Éditions F-X de Guibert, 2009), 26.

[3] Bernadot, *De l'Eucharistie à la Trinité* (Paris: Éditions du Cerf, 1920), 15.

[4] St Thérèse of Lisieux, *Story of a Soul: The Autobiography of St Thérèse of Lisieux*, trans. John Clark, O.C.D., 2nd ed. (Washington, D.C.: ICS Publications, Institute of Carmelite Studies, 1976), 14, 195.

[5] Théodelinde Dubouché, *L'Adoration au Soleil de Dieu: Fragments Spirituels*, ed. by the Sisters of Adoration for Reparation, 63.

[6] Paul VI, *Solemni Hac Liturgia* (1968), no. 26.

[7] St Peter Julian Eymard, *Adorer en Esprit et en Vérité* (Paris: Éditions F.-X. de Guibert, 2009), 93.

[8] Jean Puyo, *Dieu les a Séduits* (Paris: Desclée de Brouwer, 1994), 59.

[9] Pauline-Marie Jaricot, *L'Amour Infini dans la Divine Eucharistie* (Lyon: Imp. St Joseph), 85-86.

[10] CCC 303.

[11] St Louis-Marie Grignon de Montfort, *The Secret of Mary* (London: Catholic Way Pub., 2013), 8-9.

[12] Benedict XVI, Post-synodal Apostolic Exhortation *Sacramentum Caritatis* (2007), no. 66.

[13] *Présences Mariales, Scènes de Guerre*, Marian collection, ed. by the Marist Brothers (Varennes-sur-Allier, 1987), 95.

[14] Benedict XVI, Angelus, 10th June 2007.

[15] St Catherine de Bar, *Adorer et Adhérer* (Paris: Éditions du Cerf, 1994), 97.

[16] Bl. Dina Bélanger, *Autobiographie* (Éditions Québec, 1995), 203.

[17] This text takes up the principal themes and expressions of a lecture by Father Nicolas Buttet at Paray-le-Monial, 17th July 2007, on the theme: "Adoration for World Transformation".

[18] St Peter Julian Eymard, "Le Siècle de l'Eucharistie", LeTrès Saint Sacrement, 1864.

[19] St Thérèse of Lisieux, *Story of a Soul: The Autobiography of St Thérèse of Lisieux*, trans. John Clark, O.C.D., 2nd ed. (Washington, D.C.: ICS Publications, Institute of Carmelite Studies, 1976), 165.

[20] Paul VI, *Solemni Hac Liturgia* (1968), no. 26.

[21] Catherine de Bar, *Adorer et Adhérer* (Paris: Éditions du Cerf, 1994), 81.

[22] Fénelon, Archbishop of Cambrai, excerpt from the letter of 31st May 1707.

[23] Benedict XVI, *Address to the World of Culture*, Collège des Bernardins, Paris, 12th September 2008.

[24] St Peter Julian Eymard, *Adorer en Esprit et Vérité* (Paris: Éditions F.-X. de Guibert, 2009), 186.

[25] John Paul II, Apostolic Letter *Mane Nobiscum Domine* (2004), no. 18.

[26] St Mother Teresa, *Tu m'Apportes l'Amour: Écrits Spirituels* (Paris: Éditions du Centurion, 1975).

[27] St Peter-Julian Eymard, *Adorer en Esprit et en Vérité* (Paris: Éditions F.-X. de Guibert, 2009), 28-32.

[28] St Peter-Julian Eymard, *Adorer en Esprit et en Vérité* (Paris: Éditions F.-X. de Guibert, 2009), 23.

[29] The French word "calice" means both "calix" (also spelled "calyx": the part of a flower that surrounds the petals) and "chalice"; the word "rosée", meaning "dew", is a homonym with "rosé", the pinkish wine.–Trans.

[30] Ibid.

[31] St Faustina, *Petit Journal*, 369.

[32] John Paul II, Apostolic Letter *Dominicae Cenae: On the Mystery and Worship of the Eucharist* (1980), no. 3.

[33] Ibid.

[34] John Paul II, Letter to Bishop Houssiau for the 750th Anniversary of Corpus Christi, 28th May 1996.

[35] SK (Sketches for a Book) 903.

[36] SK 895.

[37] SK 925.

[38] St Peter Julian Eymard, *Adorer en Esprit et en Vérité* (Paris: Éditions F.-X. de Guibert, 2009), 52.

[39] Paul VI, Apostolic Letter *Solemni Hac Liturgia* (1968), no. 26.

[40] John Paul II, Encyclical Letter *Ecclesia de Eucharistia* (2003), no. 10.

[41] Bl. Dina Bélanger, *Autobiographie*, edited by the Sisters of Jesus and Mary in Canada.

[42] St Faustina, *Petit Journal*, 300.

[43] Ibid., 1484.

[44] Catherine de Bar, *Mère Mechtilde du Saint-Sacrement* (Publication Bénédictine PAX, 1922), 82.

[45] John Paul II, Message to the Faithful Gathered in the Basilica of the Sacred Heart of Montmartre, Paris, 1st June 1980, no. 4.

[46] St Peter Julian Eymard, *Oeuvres Complètes*, PR 99, 4.

[47] Ibid., CO 325, 1.

The Watchful Hour

A Scriptural Companion to Eucharistic Adoration

Fr Florian Racine

This Companion presents what the Eucharist is, what is fulfilled in the Holy Mass, what Communion and adoration are, and why and how to enter into adoration "in spirit and truth". Through Scripture, Church teaching and the works of the saints we discover that in adoring the Son, we are driven towards the Father to receive the Holy Spirit and, therefore, we become true disciples.

Split into twenty stages, adorers can reflect on one stage at a time during or after the weekly hour of adoration.

D823   ISBN 978 1 78469 192 9

Eucharistic Adoration

Prayers, Meditations and Devotions

Eucharistic Adoration includes: a special Rosary before
the Blessed Sacrament, scripture readings, prayers,
litanies, hymns, devotional images and more, all
gathered together to inspire prayer before our Lord.
It also contains the rite of Exposition and Benediction.

D757   ISBN 978 1 86082 825 6

A Quarter Hour Before the Blessed Sacrament

Fold-out Prayer

This wallet card has been made as an aid to adoration of the Blessed Sacrament. Its size makes it simple to carry and to give to people who are spending this special time with the Lord. Written as a conversation between the person in prayer and Jesus, the text is meant to help people pass 15 minutes quietly reflecting on the love of Jesus, present in the Blessed Sacrament. It invites them to speak with him and to open their hearts and lives to his power. It's perfect for putting at the back of the church or for use during adoration.

A Quarter Hour Before the
Blessed Sacrament

HANA ΙC   ΛΗΨΙC ΧC

To please Me, dear child, it is not necessary to know much; all that is required is to love Me much, to be deeply sorry for ever having offended Me and desirous of being ever faithful to Me in future.

PC82 ISBN 506 0 13900 052 9